Devotional

DEDICATED

TO

MARK

LANEGAN

TABLE OF CONTENTS

Leaving Music
Long have you comforted me with your touch honey,
but I must leave your fingers
Do not trail them behind me
like little ghosts of pianos.
take them and touch your own shoulder,
tenderly.
Find your guitar and see,
see the vibrations I left in your room?
Keep them circling.
Too long have I strived,
reaching with one hand that always seems to be
cut up.
reaching upwards
toward streaking skies.
I'm turning from you baby,
my boots in your room leaving dust.
I'm barefoot now,
cut those up too.
part of my god complex.

The guitar:
Spanish ebony,
¾ scale,
22 frets.
Gutstrings that soothed my
bruised nails,
warmth emanated from it.
I pounded it on the fucking street and gave it a new soundhole.

I was a kid,
raped and beat and left on the street and I
took to you,
the first woman who moved in some way
I approved of.
Raped and bruised and beat on the corner of the street,
Love you kissed my hands and they hurt.
I came home with a new body
In the kingdom of heaven it is your birthright,
I came home self-actualized
and chased you with my burning fingers baby
I leave that wood behind me.

I'm on Haight and I
see my baby niece alone
on the street,
someone left her there,
just left her to go buy
dope in the park.
I pick her up, she's
fussing and anxious,
but she can see that I'm
okay.
I put her in the car and drive to fourth.
I go inside and everything's okay,
I'm cooking chicken and my mom and
brothers are there, it's all okay
Then someone goes
"Where's Janey?
Bro, where's Janey?"
I left her in the car.

I wanted to tell you this baby, wanted you to
help me babe.

But I'm on the street in blue jeans
weeping without you.

Remember in the army?
It was dark and I'd come back from
sand
where I ripped the
throats from the children of the enemy
and left their homes hollow and empty.
I came back and you were in my tent.
the sand was painted blue by the full moon,
and your clothes were hollow and empty.

Love me right over my green shirt and my long hair and right over
everything, boy,
cause you smoothed your body down on both my eyes
and all of a sudden everything was pale, pale white.
When I awoke there was a tattoo on my gun
and I shot it for years.
I was a widower for you.

burned my palms for you.

I fought and fought
in every bar known to man
I played a Spanish guitar
and after every show I threw up
I am eternally busting through the back door
running in to a cook smoking
nearly dropping the guitar
clutching my stinging fingers
I climbed through an electric fence drunk once
to get away from cops
humming Chan Chan
and now my fingers are golden

don't cry, remember when we
walked hand in hand and you were golden too
your golden boy you raised
smiling on a Sunday
with his hand in yours girl
sleeping with a notebook
I could go on forever
but I need to leave you
I'm gonna keep talking and talking and talking
and one day it's all just gonna fade away

Keep your guitar going for me, honey.
Play crested hens for me.

Montana
Tonight I like my shadow.
Something sympathetic about painted-black curls on
crackerjack concrete.

There's an airplane wheeling,
golden in the
sky
like an asteroid encroaching ever-
larger in the
high
frame of two towering
spires, sent to
give me a very personal and holy death.

It passes, and I reflect
down the street. I reflect on
rural places with many trees.
Places that have cradled my brain
and torn the
flesh of my long
walking legs.

There are mountains that,
to this day, will
press their peaks
into the
soft purple of my
sky and make me sweat. Make me
eager for
dusty green roads and
babbling brooks.

The hills around my home are ones
I return and fall into.
My
conscious mind fades
and I
sluice them in sleep. Then
with wild hair and big hands
they lay
me in a

pool of
fresh milked constellations.

I turn a corner into crowds, seeing more of
Kalispell and wanting more cold train cars.
From Livingston the freights float by
They're fat like whales.
Livingston must be big rock candy mountain.

My brutalistic migration patterns
Like a bird in spring whose heart is south
Summers are in some orange grove,
and Montana in the winter.

Montana is very deep.

I fall through apartments,
dorms and flats.
I fall through farms,
The tops of dimly lit hay racks.
Many safe and warm dives,
A cosmic tower with near Alaskan dark
And the northern lights
And falling snow all about.

It's winter,
But going up the steps and taking my key
I'm struck by tonight's heat.
nearly springlike.

On the second floor I rent out on darlington drive, I wrench the window open to hear the shouts.
I see a band playing through the smoke and pretty people dancing
out loud.
This is one of few suburbs I've liked.

Smelling good meat and seeing good skies,
I'm thinking this is my paradigm for
summertime. Tonight, the fifth of January in Montana winter. And
next year I'll be cold and in Livingston and I'll want for summer and
I'll think of tonight.

Tonight, I like the way my mountains look,
black against fields
once full of rye.

Normandy
On the beach at Normandy with her,
In the belly of a flaming nazi tank.
This blood dripping
keeps putting my cigarette out
I sigh.
Taking a drag, my elbows shoved into
The steel corners, I suck the smoke and
wince a little.

Letting her hair down,
Ana's bangs curl all around and
stick to her face like sweat.
I can't stretch my legs and
she tries and knocks her foot on an
ammo box.
Her suspenders are down around her hips.
My shirt is stained red.

Composing myself, running
my hair back,
there's something hot and sticky in it.
This blood I say, pawing at it.
She hands me a campaign poster,
the colors on it frighten me.
I fold the thing and
give it to my wallet to keep.
You'll vote for me then?

Sloshing over to the porthole I see some
Americans,
they don't see us though.

I clear my throat.
Would you like to marry me?
She dances to herself,

she's no james brown but she's alright.

something tells me I need to leave,
I can climb out,
there's nothing to stop me.

But something else says that
to leave her here with all her friends
and the life of a genocider spilling from every crack
would be
cruel.

So even though I know she drink the stuff,
I stay.

The Hills

It's four of us chasing the sun

Stone cliffs shot through with sagebrush rise
from ravines.
The wind carries crushed flowers
through the AC.

There are great animals here, dark backs
heaving. They are the hills, and
their terracotta spines split the silver burlap
purple sky.

A fence post arrives,
stands brokeback.
Crippled by
us and our car in another life.
The splintered wood is stark and harsh,
and from the valley a
bell tolls.

The words begin now, they fall frenzied,
dripping from our lips,
running down our chins,
soaking our shirts.
We are slavering dogs, repenting
at the moon.

The last sunlight refracts through our windshield
and
dies in our corneas.
The hills stand up and begin to walk.

Rot (Tom Mix)

1.

wine-drunk on your unbuttoned shirt and the
wind in your long hair and
the way the hibiscus talk.
stop a minute and
the leaves'll open your face and the
dirt'll weep at your bare feet as Mary Magdalene.
no, as Tom Mix.
and you'll feel real at peace.

2.

When you look around and see only beautiful things,
you know there is a corpse beneath your feet.
Grown over with purple wildflowers
and the red muscle boiled, painted, against the grass.
But rotting.

3.

there's a rot in these trees
there's a rot in this ground
there's a rot in my step
there's a rot goin on

The Band
It was cold.
We were to fight the horde that day,
and I came to him at dawn.
He shivered and cried,
his hair was all down in his face.
I gave him the black band that kept my brow clear,
and the red spilled about my cheekbones as I kissed him.
-

Through the spears and
the hail of arrows, his jaw was set
and his blond beard bloody.
He hacked a dervish,
his eyes shone for me.
There were so many,
and I could not see the blades that cut me.

Under Lights

In the daytime,
under a multiplicity of lights,
we section each other off like
cattle, chop ourselves up.
dreams of dead fish at market.
/

The slimming shirt, the appealing dress
/

But when the lights come down,
I'll see what we really are.
In death I am born again and in
life I am failing,
but when the lights come down, all
I see is the scratch that brings to
flower
my breast,
bleeding sex.
And when the lights come down
our bodies expand, exhale to
cover the dark, I see us
fat and soft.
I'll love you there.
I see us black and wrinkled,
I love you there
I see us lost to the night.
I will love you then.

No Blade

You stitch the shoes up because
they fall
apart.

a few years under your
belt, you see the way
things rot
around you, the way you
dully claw at them,
fat bloody sausages for
fingers

So you strip.
Naked as a monk, just
the ramshackle chucks,
some scratched eyeglasses,
a guitar on your back.
You sink into the hills,
elope with your words
to a barrel. Think
yourself enlightened with
the splinters
in your ass

and you're happy-
running around singing.
tacking the poems to your lovers bed.
drinking on
mountaintops,
wind combs your
hair and beard,
flies away with it.
dancing on the
roof with the starlight
rotating around your hips.

Contentment

For a long time

When your friends start to die,

you rage. Burning you say
No more. Those that still
stand, you leave them,
muttering
penance.

You fight. Not the killer,
there is no fighting it.
no blade
with which
to
clash.
But
you war and you flame and
when your beard is white you
look and
they are gone.

The ones you left behind,
those tall trees.
The forest behind
grandmothers cabin,
oh,
the berry bushes-
they are gone.

"Are we just houses for the angels?"

and you walk the valley of your mountain
with a cask of rotted wine and rags about your feet.

Fly West
Maybe I fly
west with the
girl at the bar who looks a little
familiar and leans against the door and
smiles when I walk in.
I'd wear two guns low and a
scarf round my neck and I'd shoot
bullets through barn doors that
rustle in the green grass on the other side.
the clouds would be gray and we'd bust the doors down
and she'd have a derringer on her hip
and be smarter than me and
we'd be on a train when
the people from the bank would come and paint the
coalcar with my brains but she'd
get away with just
my last name.

Spider

Wrapping a spider in a flower.
From her many eyes flow poison tears,
they flow down my flower down it's petals and
burn upon my skin so pale
And I cry too,
"I do not want to eat you."
"I do not want to eat you no more."

You were in my living room.
From your two eyes flow silver tears,
I turn my collar up and step away.
And I cry too,
"Please do not hurt me
"Please do not hurt me no more."

Stop Running Song (1.)
All up and down the black sea's coast
I cut myself on black rocky roads
Great big, gnarled and gray toes spread before me
in the shape of oriental fans
Ape feet slapping in the rain.
/
It had been like this for a few years
when I was sat on the tram,
My eyes were tangled, underneath
and inside of
my hood,
and I drew them back when I saw his face.
/
Back and forth under
dripping eaves,
I reach into the air and
pluck a leaf
blown from the weeping willow tree.

I Protect These Woods
Despite all I am born!
The flesh is gold
The flesh is silver,
The flesh is cast as a beautiful receiver.

Torn from the throes of this
dirty
orgasm,
ripped from my skin as
capillaries shatter.
broken,
the Sun
boils my blood
and sets aflame my throat.

Crosslegged, emaciated,
I lift to the
roiling storm and
God
begins to swim in my cheekbones.
Not all children cast in
shadows
do evil.

I am born again
I am a black goat
Standing by trees so dark,
Ribs cracking like a rotten gunwale,
forehead bleeding,
bleating
a prayer
unto this mountain.

Lyrics to a Song I'll Never Play Live
fisher man
that's a nice gun on your hip
fisher man
will you take me on your trip
through grassy lakes and glass of river and wheeling thoughts
throughout
follow an arc of sacred country,
snakes were gods and we had no house
to the villain you showed a final hand
one that defended the boy I loved at the time
and then you said I was a man

fisher man
that's a nice gun on your hip
fisher man
will you take me on your trip
I tried to keep you from slipping into ponds of wine along the way
but I was so young and you were so strong and sometimes you'd
bathe anyway
you've not fired your gun at no man
and you couldn't hit the barn door really
you'd only put it on kitchen tables while we ate and
eyed the door.

but bullets have always gone
where I asked them to
I'd shoot them all at cars on the road
to make your mind like new

fisher man
you're kind of like my brother
fisher man
but I still love my mother

Untitled
a dream;
White birches cutting an image, shapely, fell from her red dress. Lifting herself from the curb to the dusty old van that I'm loading with cables and speakers, this was a chance arrangement.
She had mick jaggered her face up and she walked the part.
Hey Mary, what's up?
Not much, need a ride though.
Hop in.
...
Back in texas my mother said William you need to find yourself a nice girl, this woman is too smart, she's got her a tongue that cut silver
She looks down her nose at that long tall greasefire swaying down the driveway
But you need to learn I reckn
...
Southern-lady-exemplified is wrong so I pay her no attention.
Standing in the kitchen Mary's buttering bread and I'm trying to break the ice but I feel like I'm just brushing the glaciers goddam teeth.
I said something, I don't remember what, but the clouds broke open and there's that smile I'd been fishing for
"Let's go swimming Billy"
...
I chased after her, never quite catching up,
to my immense pleasure.
She was in a black bikini, muscles rippling like a big cat as she sprinted to the pool
Catch up!
No! I yelped, throwing my shirt to the side
She made a running jump at the fence, clinging to the side
I did the same, and it teetered
Crashed
All fifteen tall green feet of it, on to the top of the pool.
We howled with laughter and hauled it off, and slipped our bodies into the water like gore knives into a tunas gut.
Budley and Daniel and my father joined us some minutes later, sitting
Shoulder to shoulder like a biological freak.
They're jostling among themselves in the water like puppies but I'm anxious for almost-empty water so I say
You guys oughta get out on the river, you're missing all the good fish,

and I pointed to the goldens
and salmon
and cutthroat
that swam, magnificent, in the sky,
And I cast a knowing glance at Mary, my compatriot in coyotehood as
the brothers realize what's going on

Good Day

We are so different now,
it is so hard to reach you.
You stoop deep into the valley we swore to leave,
while I labor in the mountains now.
Our words meet and fight
like boys in the churchyard,
the poor light of the restaurant
makes us look ill.
We sweat like fish on a block and flit our eyes,
I cannot stay here, no no
I have to leave.
You reach and take my scarf in your hand,
it tears.
I collapse in my car, panting and gagging.
I go home and change,
put my hair down .
My deodorant mixes with the incense and it smells like
cherry soda pop.
-

Then we go and sing and dance
in the market square.
This new group, we
pile electricity and fire
in a heap, douse it with
water and shoot it to the sky.
Run!
Gun!
Chant!
Speak Slant!
In the darkness rises a strange sun,
in the market square!
I shove my hips and
clap my hands
and shout and snort
and holler and jump
and sing loud and turn my eyes
up to the bright night
and there's this torn cloth round my neck!

Thirteen Rivers

dancing in the living room
hips swinging and wine spilling and
thirteen children courting thirteen children
thirteen rivers behind thirteen smiling teeth,
eleven bodies gone down to the store to
get something

I remember you, collapsed in a chair
heaving from love,
thirteen dams have almost broken and you're
smiling up at me

dancing in the living room
I see that thirteen dark rivers have
flooded the burial pits of your eyes,
and I see you twisting and
breaking inside
I see you
smiling at me,
shouting-
Love Me!

Your Revolution
White cherries grow
where you used to lie
blossom hair thrown
side to side

there were stark raving cowboys
with their foots on the walls
bop played on the streets
all the women wore shawls
on that night

two old friends teetered down Roman street
I danced with a girl named parakeet
the friends pushed each other against the wall
just like the feet of the cowboys
all the women wore shawls
on that night.

Church and Chapelwaite
Hold one hand in the
other, and
cry while you arch your back.
If you nurse it baby I'll kiss it,
and one long day we'll
take it and we'll
kill their children with it.
Rise to me boy and I will rinse you,
and we will come from under cold stones,
from valleys and deserts,
we will come from the city and the country
and the church and the chapelwaite

Alaska

1.
I feel to find the
channels of a space,
the rivers that run underfoot,
underground,
beneath the bricks of this church.
Black man fired from the boat who hates it
here
Table waiter with marks up and down his arms, fat in
polyester rolling down his frame,
tears barely contained by
magic brown eyes that are a prison.
2.
I'm at a time in my life where
I am shedding.
My inhibitions have slid off me
like water off Venus,
In small rooms with streetlight
through the shades,
I see myself in ten years.
In someone's bed,
moonlight slicking off my
hips and collapsing at their feet.
3.
Some bitch insults my newly discarded influences.
I go and gather up all the
violence I've scattered across the land,
juice it, and put it in a
shot for her to take.
4.
I see the mountains and feel as if
I am at God's feet.
Maybe in another life I could've loved you,
Camelot.
But in the hotel safe's crags and valleys,
left by a hundred thousand guns,
packets of photos,
cases of heroin,
I think no.
Probably not.

Why?
Why do I dance so
where is my partner
Why do my toes throb
you do not trod them

Blackbird blackbird
the shock you gave
lingers still
Bluebird bluebird
leaned there on the windowsill

The lover who pushes me to the
edge of the bed, but now leaves empty sheets beneath her
who leaves me teetering still
who leaves me wearing dark glasses to hide the tears in her eyes.

Jungletown
When I was in the forest,
I held you off with two sputtering torches.
You were something ugly,
moving between trees,
dark but not shapeless.
Oh, not shapeless
my love.

I turned rapidly
and the lights went out.
Instantly
you were at my throat.

Could you take a many toothed maw
and kiss the gently stinking thick
of its flesh?
Ignore the rot of a cornucopia down its throat?

In the morning as the
sun comes through the leaves,
I shine a light over my shoulder
and see a shivering bambi
in a bed of mush,
with big eyes and gumteeth.
And little baby is looking only to me.

This now, is jungletown.

Cropdust
The heart of the forest, the heart of the sea;
the thin black vein of the world naked before me
The blood of a thousand dancers laid
bare
throat shouted raw,
unhinged jaw.
a great wide neck, and us walking the throbbing artery,
an artery pulsing with every love we've ever lost
Every woman I asked to marry me
Every time my mother made me cry,
every time the records she gave me
opened my eyes.
I will never find a word cruel enough,
tender enough,
Oh lord, there is nothing
The profane beauty that coursed our skin,
the leaves,
that sky,
all of it.
The entire fucking thing,
thumping in our ears.
while a crop dusting plane goes by,
over our heads in the nighttime.
Orange billowing clouds,
a pocketful of lye
A crop duster over our heads in the nighttime,
and god nude on a platter before me

Total Midnight Dark
Every day I do this.
Crawl these streets.
Cut myself on angular steel.
The air is completely still.
I stalk the rooftops and it swells,
stagnates so that the
hordes of addicts cling to me like flies
as I pass them by,
buzzing vaguely below my waist.
Sometimes as I'm moving fast and low
to the ground,
the buildings despite their soupy
obfuscation
seem to glow,
not the structures themselves but
the image in my mind.
This happens in such a way that
I decouple from
the anchors of
the slums,
and I'm recognizing the city
completely
within myself, and the
skyscrapers blaze with a throwing
turning luminescence and I'm
still moving about the city blocks but they
run together, they become only the colors that
click and pulse behind my eyes.
As I move unnaturally through gates and over fences
in the total midnight dark.

Communist Afterlife
A blade between my ribs,
my belly opened for all the gas station
parking lot to see.
And blood runs hot n sweaty cross
my teeth while some pig says it was
likely drug related ma'am you know them fuckin country boys n what
they cook out there
and he says this and my unadulterated blood run
clean and beautiful across his shiny
black shoes and I
open my eyes upon a star
and piggy's heart stops and he drops
and I roll laughing, shining my light down
and it goes through the broken faces of
the broken people there at the shell station
and like prisms they cast brilliance from their
smiles that dances
divine

Portrait One

Big silver rings, faded
Long willowy scarfs
and eyeglasses
that you look perfect in
I, I may be smelling of spit
I may be thin haired and big bellied and blue around my edges
I may keep a big red hand on a little silver gun and
watch backdoors for fun
but if I could write you a second of the street we walked on at night
I'd be happy.

For M
and there's a man who hides his face,
standing still like he's tied to a mast,
beeswax stuffed in his ears. He's all done
up in black and a frown and sweat off heavy brow breaks on the
hardwood.
and the ignorant don't see that the sun is bright or that fire dresses in
dark.
they never do bro

Gibraltr Square (2.)
Living with him on Gibraltr square
I learned about tables

Sat between the cracked blue corner and the scaly green window
I stared through an empty notebook at the marred rosewood
Living with him on Gibraltr square
I learned about empty notebooks
I eternally thought about free tides and raging black waves, under
which in scant and poorly lit shoals I thrived

On Gibraltr square
I lived and died as the sun set and rose
Beside my empty notebook I kept a vase of roses,
lilies and lavender, with sprigs of lupine and rye that sprung and
grew through like bones clinging to a hill after the animal has died.

Gibraltr square with him
At first I'd sit with my work and take toast and tea, and taste whatev-
er flower scent came to me
But soon in that bare room above Gibraltr square with him I lost all
appetite
I took nothing.
But the flowers were like a drug and I didn't need anything to eat.
They were sweet like a headache and I was drunk and it was enough.

I wrote maybe seven words in six months and slept none.

On Gibraltr square with him I took flowers to eat and I did not sleep.

The City, The Town
Loneliness consumed us.

Bottle cap with the tooth marks clinks on the walk.
You told me that there was a river inside you,
and I was the flotsam.
I told you that I came to this as a way to stay sane.
That I'm one essay away from death,
That I saved myself with a poem three years ago and haven't looked
back since.

Painful as it may be,
loneliness consumed us on sixth street.

I've been in the city a week.
We caught waves,
they all crashed on you at once
and you smiled, crazed.
You told me how happy it made you
to see me in the water, laughing
You light up your pipe.

Loneliness consumed us,
and we realized we wouldn't
make the beach in time.
Still, you say, this is how we live forever.

Through the markets,
up the streets,
are women whose bodies are to be
broken open at the breastbone
like lobster tails and the grease sucked out.

Men who are long and blond and to be taken
and juiced like lemonade
all over the street.

I'm aware these sentiments are wicked.

Still we remain.

consumed by loneliness and already beginning to feel the rain,

You say I'm welcome to stay.
No, I've got that thing up a state and besides
I've gotta tell mom what you say.

But fourth street siddhartha baby,
next time I'm through it'll be to stay or
not to see you at all.

A river runs through me and it is you,
your grooves will last forever.

Loneliness consumes us and we can't make the beach,
but this is how we live forever, right?

Streetcar
Old lover in an old streetcar.
last time I saw her she was screaming.
with a warm glance my ears pop.
a little blood on the blacktop
Freezes quick.
With the sexiest flick of a wrist I've ever seen,
she leans and shouts
Have I been loved?

Your Second Revolution
Dress me in horn music
pulsing on the bricks

in the theater of obsessiveness
we sat it was full I thought of you when they kissed
I watched as they fell sweaty from their grace
We're still friends, aren't we?

Wind Chimes

Wind chimes put their hands on my thighs-
open the second story and I will fly.
when the dog dreams,
he cries.
The drydocks were my home.
When does it come in?
When does it come in?
I picked leaves from
the blossoms of one tree.
I designed a flower for you made of these.
At last your hand was on my hand
and it is gone again.
Your carriage trundling up the rain drunk street
to the shining house of Komalpreet.

Signet
The world becomes real before you,
and the things that went unsaid
have entered the room

Pool
water pool in the dark
eyes scared side to side.
three silver glints in a spraying night
stand up, touch me
on my legs and feet-
some girls are laughing,
maybe nervously I don't know.
trace my ass with
nails on you like coral,
the waves and waves of
licking your lips
lash me against you,
finally exiting through a
veil of the
hundred thousand bottom teeth showing
birthed to a hot night shivering

I Can't Sew Myself Up

I can't sew myself up,
I'm not a
nurse for the orchids.
the uniforms I've
set for myself are dust at my feet,
and ahead a dust storm is spinning.
tonight I have broken down at the altar of
another human being. The gods who ignored me
continued to do so.

A Gunshot Rings Out

1.
Sharon Stone spreads her legs and
with a gunshot that sings I am
wide awake.
The distance between my bedsheets
and your
imaginary waist at the window
covered with crass speed,
the last of whatever
dream I had
leaks out my hands and feet and
instantly my arm is around me.
one hand
one hip.
2.
Standing there another second,
and your
golden light dies in the blinds,
a gunshot sings and it's
ten thirty at night
(but Indian summer).
The colors outside are
winding out,
coming down
from the
high
flourishes, strives and
drama of early eveningtime.
A gunshot shouts and I've
slept through the
garden of pink and purple
Time and again.
3.
Leaving a
movie theater of dead blues
in the glass, ebbing,
I shatter down the hallway.
I eat off last months plate and finish
the millenniums bread, break
off to a spot on the couch
to take a needlefull of thought while a

shot moans loud.
4.
Am I letting you slam my car door shut,
just to have to see you cry into that
headscarf I love?
A gunshot sings around and it's the one
with brown tooling, and gold stitches, and
silver paisley,
and when you wear it with your black glasses I know you're the pret-
tiest bitch out there and I go crazy,
all with gunfire springing on the walls and fucking off.
I lay there a while and
just for a while.
7.
That's enough for one
insomniatic spell
enough of
the pill that makes me mad.
So I run back to bed.
Gunshots ring around
like little dogs
barking on the
dark ground outside,
I lunge under the covers
while this
great looking lead cracks on my windowsill.

Dove
hey dove,
talk all day long.
come night, I'll take you
where I'm from.
I think fucking is too much,
but it's too cold
not to
wear my blankets, dove.

You
Outside the clouds are a deep
navy,
and they streak high above the rooftops
and pulsing stars
and baking asphalt.

The television has cooked my
grandmother's brain, she lies with big white
eyes and a leaking skull in the next
room with a blanket to her chin.
I am at the table with my notebook,
drawing back a thin film from the night
to reveal dark raw skin,
throbbing.

So long have I said
"You",
It is the most beautiful knife in my blanket
and I use it deftly.

Tonight when a fly buzzes,
I look up and around.

I burst from the foyer to
the walk.

Wolves
The wolves I collect
are all lepers and thieves

the dancing fool, crying
always

the old one whose smile drips with
disease onto it's paws

and the orphan black genius with opal eyes

I walk behind them.
they're in some fairytale and I'm just
the idiot that feeds them.

Kingsname (3.)

Out on coastal streets with
sunshine in my leaves
and streetsigns
with names I can't pronounce,
that lead nowhere but
away from here.

I see the church and cross the street,
hover at the door thinking I might get smited.
daddy would've cut me for this.

I kneel in the benches and
halfway through the second song I
Break down
And cry and cry and cry

And there's a voice
Seeming to say, choose.
Now,
please.

A muscle I didn't know I have
flexes darkly
The ashes they spread on me are
black, and look like the sea
where I'm originally from.

They go up my nose and my legs
just can't stop
shaking.

Up and down the black sea's coast,
someone's name on my lips and a partial
oratory scattered through my pockets
in
snips.

First Month
It was the first month of the year
the machines were moving faster than
the thing my broken child's mind prayed to.
my god had hidden itself
beneath strangers fingernails.
I was submerged in
swimming pools instead of
bookshelves.
there was a serial killer in seattle again,
and every day an author died.
-

I had some business so I went out in front of
the rising sun,
it was red and brilliant like a bloody wound
and pissed out nineteen rays of salmon light,
and on each one a naked woman rode a brindle horse

Gray Ghost/Hill to Hell

I asked if I could borrow the
drawing I made of you as a gift;
just for the night. To have some
kind of face in my room.

I went to hang it with a
golden nail, and
I couldn't

then a gray ghost of you appeared
laying on my ceiling
she floated,
and she hung it,
and she
dropped into me and
told me to love it

the whole time, I was reaching backwards to touch
your face,
the one I made for you to have and me
to covet

finally, she left through the
light fixture and everything
...
shook like a bird.

you shook like a bird in
the empty night that would never be full

and you shook like a bird when you
tasted the food in heaven

and I remember you
shook like a bird at the thought
that
the hill to hell may be diamond and jade

but when we one hand danced and your hair was on the floor,
your legs were so steady.

Boy With Red Wings
boy with red wings,
once suspended among
kestrels and stars

boy with red wings, they're uh
they're poking through your shirt

boy with red wings,
climb that roof and
kiss the feet
of the man who used to
hold your hand

one hand takes the blame
the other makes a promise not to beat anyone

the mouth to feed doesn't eat very often,
boy with red wings

Song for A
Beauty so thin
Beauty so stretched
I could barely see it
The only thing I ever saw
Was the sunlight glinting off it

Hours swell to years
And the mourning doves are still talking
Talking of your love

How she woke everyone
Running through the forest
Spitting behind her back
Naked as the early morning sun
That dressed itself and went away from her

I was in that word
I was ready to die by that word

I heard her wailing above the fiddles
That you were going to die by the sword

Sunday Morning

there's always something watching
from the closet.
guitars are tables on
Sunday morning.

The bathtub is chirping,
and
Skinny wings,
bottled up flings,
are not yours to master
in the morning.

On Sunday morning,
to grieve and banish misfortune,
I would adopt the innocence I've
so long ignored.

There's not a single war or death
or blood vessel exploding,
but I want to fall from your grace
more and more.

Tear down the walls of your house
while away you work,
paint it with the dust of my luggage

I wanna fall from your grace so fucking bad.
why are you so fucking sad all the time?

There's someone killing themselves every Sunday morning.

Grace Unthinkable
They said things that shocked me
I expressed disbelief and was treated kindly.
They did nothing to teach me, they did
nothing to change a mind,
but they did,
and it was mine.

Reeling from the way they thought,
I smile between trees on a newly green street.
Nineteen feet from home I fall,
blood sugar low,
lay down on the warm sidewalk.

the sun sets and the suicides rise like a great red dune in the sky.

I Hate Poets
why don't you want me
why are you always so bright
why do my hands fall away from you if I
trace your thighs

I'm so tired of words
let me touch you
I know no names or faces
you'll never know how I feel

god I hate poets

I Fell In Love With Hawaii

I sat on the shore and watched the waves roll in,
at every new star that undressed itself for me I jumped:
"this is it"
the chronic oversaturation of
propagandic capitalist media is leading a
hyper isolated proletariat to
post ironic depressive detachment and I'm
sitting on the shore and I haven't had my first kiss
-

I could feel suicide in the air
like a bashful prince
with his cock in his hand
down the beach two people
are loving on each other,
honeymooning at world's end
it begins to rain so soft it feels like
little fish
I sat on the shore laden with sex and suicide and the little fish kissed
me and said
it's gonna be alright
it's gonna be alright
-

and as I retreat inside
my mind remains,
to go walking on two feet
across beaches and black swells and the
holy site where I felt the world fall from beneath me
all I was ever interested in was
putting things in your head that comforted you.
pornography about the ocean,
erotica about your soul
-

the infrastructure has collapsed and
wars are popping up like
bands that don't have a fucking thing on us,
and I haven't been back to Hawaii since the
cows started to die.
sometimes in my head I still sit like that though, and ask:
are there still cartoon gods behind every blue cloud?
when the stars get naked does your heart still pound?
do bats still face shore while the

wind pushes them away?
is the moonlight still laying on top of the water like it's lazy?

The Bioptic Theory

Pain n playshure he say,
he say it
leaning in now-
spins a circle with his hand smiling;

fer evry kiss on th lips,
someone dead in th desrt
yr dad, he doesnt know ewe,
but yew are still lovin him

a lit-tle baby is born,
holy n the golden light of
her ma,
and then n old man dies
alone wif his wife gone t
th store

evry stolen night beneath
willer trees,
oooh yung luvers,
a rebellion is quelled n the red red red red
red blood
ov heroes

here he puts his head on his arm,
and the rings of people lean ever deeper into the lamplight,
rapt

Fer every earth
quake on th hips, a
soonami ov th
roiling, drowning mind

July
I went July not knowing you.
What fields have you wandered through?

Did you leave music behind?
I did, and after one night collapsed before it.

In travel have you seen the same things
I behold every night alone before the TV?

It barks softly and on the back porch mosquitoes aloft,
carrying brand new diseases to you and to the yellowhawks.

Imagist's Hymn
the bulwark has collapsed
play amongst it's stony bones

the war has ended long ago
soldiers sell flowers now

my hands are on my knees and
my feet are in a bowl of hot water
and I smile like this
when my friends come through the door

children laugh down the village streets
and in my little house through the window we kiss each other's
cheeks

instruments feel clumsy in my hands
and I look up with a little fright

god, you're all as beautiful as the
day we lost

windmill made of paper turns in the warm breeze
our laughter begins to separate my soul from my thoughts

all the things we left unsaid
are laying down together in the dark yard

a hundred thousand years ago

You Are All That I Am
twice was I kissed by the needle
before by a woman or man
except for the lips of grandfather
and grandmother
dry and cracked and saying
you are all that I am

in the bowels of the caverns
in the ballasts of the fear
I carried only the weapon of God
singing forever in my ears

and when I drank from the enemy's hand, I said
you are all that I am

when the body grows weak
for a woman you do not need
your mind melts like mush
and there will come some
love

springing across the fields and
hopping in cricket air
please enough to tell her
you are all that I am

in hotel rooms
sick and weeping
tears that feel like
diarrhea down your face
am I strong enough to wash
the fear from my life

you are all that I am

you are all that I am, little dog
you are all that I am, little mouse
you are all that I am, big whale
you are all that I am, empty house
you are all that I am, Crying In The Shower
you are all that I am, girls on trains

you are all that I am, Handmade Mugs
you are all that I am, little brother

I refuse anymore to pretend
that I die tonight
I'm going to live forever
I know that tonight
grandmother, believe me
grandfather, I'm sorry
I know that you know
you are all that I am

Blue Tuesday
Leave golden hour,
I take blue tuesday.

The time of day when white blossoms fade and
droop and are lavender blue.
When the wood of the trunk becomes
midnight navy,
and the bushes dark dusty
pink, and the fence
coated with a thick black syrup,
gravied over with bluegrass juice.

and I would dress in denim and wade through oceans to come and
get you.

Looking for Your Love
I walked down the street in a storm
dressed in a western shirt
yours

lightning cracked in the sky and I let myself in

here's the the tomatoes
I'm setting them on the table
what's the score?

then salty tears burned
where his strong old hands held my head
and he told me that he hadn't done enough for me
and while the wind ran up the brown hills outside
and slid down fast
my hair began to grow until it looked
just how it does
when the next story starts

THANKS TO:

Teo Bicchieri
Teresa Bicchieri
Noemie Bicchieri
Paolo Bicchieri
Lucie Pereira
Trina Lanegan
Mark Lanegan
Shelley Lanegan
Paul Coppin
Floy Hotarek
Bill Hotarek
Leo Robison
Nathaniel Arango
Andrew Byrd
Jampa Dorge
Wesley Eisold
Amy Lee
Barrett Martin

Communist Afterlife, First Month, Blue Tuesday, and Boy With Red Wings first published in Heartworm Reader Issue No. 2, Heartworm Press, 2023

The Band first published in Q+A: A Queerzine, 2024

David Coppin Lanegan is a musician and writer living in the desert in
Central Washington.

Find him on Instagram at @williambillybilliam

Find his band at @_theblackvelvetband_

And his music and book distribution at @snakemusicrecords

Email: velvetbandblack@gmail.com